0603695

W9-AVL-800

E 1021 0201193 3

ON LINE

Batter Up!

You Can Play Softball

by Nick Fauchald
illustrated by Ronnie Rooney

Special thanks to our advisers for their expertise:

Brian McCall, Director of Communications
ASA/USA Softball, Oklahoma City, Oklahoma

Susan Kesselring, M.A., Literacy Educator
Rosemount–Apple Valley–Eagan (Minnesota) School District

PICTURE WINDOW BOOKS
Minneapolis, Minnesota

Editorial Director: Carol Jones

Managing Editor: Catherine Neitge

Creative Director: Keith Griffin

Editor: Jill Kalz

Story Consultant: Terry Flaherty

Designer: Joe Anderson

Page Production: Picture Window Books

The illustrations in this book were created with acrylics.

Picture Window Books

5115 Excelsior Boulevard

Suite 232

Minneapolis, MN 55416

877-845-8392

www.picturewindowbooks.com

Printed in the United States of America.

Library of Congress Cataloging-in-Publication Data

Fauchald, Nick.

Batter up! You can play softball / by Nick Fauchald ; illustrated by Ronnie Rooney.

p. cm. — (Game day)

Includes bibliographical references and index.

ISBN 1-4048-1152-4 (hardcover)

1. Softball—Juvenile literature. I. Title: Batter up! II. Title: You can play softball.

III. Rooney, Ronnie, ill. IV. Title.

GV881.F38 2006

796.357′8—dc22   2005004268

Softball is a game played by people of all ages, all over the world. The rules are simple: Two teams take turns at bat and in the field. They try to score points, called runs, by hitting the ball and running around the bases. The team that has scored the most runs by the end of the game wins.

"Hey, we're going to be late for the game!"
Your friend Hannah stops by your house on
the way to the field. It's time to leave for your
fast-pitch softball game!

You grab your glove and softball, then bike
to the softball field. Your team, the Muskrats,
is warming up. Coach hits ground balls to the
infield, while James and Tracy play catch in
the outfield. You join them.

4

A softball field is divided into the infield and outfield. The first, second, and third basemen stand near their bases in the infield. The shortstop stands between second and third base. The pitcher stands on the pitching mound and pitches to the catcher behind home plate. Three outfielders stand in the outfield beyond the bases.

5

"Batter up!" the umpire says. The visiting team, the Cardinals, gets to bat first. Your pitcher, Kris, pitches the ball over home plate. The batter swings and misses. "Strike one!" yells the umpire.

Kris pitches again. WHACK! The ball sails into the outfield. A fly ball! You hold up your glove and watch the ball drop into it. Great catch!

Softball and baseball are very similar, but in softball, the pitcher throws the ball underhand. Each game is divided into innings. In each inning, both teams get to bat until they get three outs.

7

When catching a fly ball, position yourself under the ball. Hold both of your arms up in the air. Watch the ball drop into your glove and squeeze the glove shut. Use your free hand to cover the glove so the ball doesn't fall out. When fielding a ground ball, move your body in front of the ball, bend your knees, and place your glove on the ground. Watch the ball roll into your glove.

The Muskrats need two more outs to take their turn at bat. The next Cardinal batter hits a ground ball to Cori, near third base. She scoops up the ball and throws it to Jon at first base for the second out.

The next Cardinal hits a ground ball to Jon at first base. Jon bends down to grab the ball and steps on the base for the third out. Now it's the Muskrats' turn to bat.

You are the first batter for the Muskrats. You grab your helmet and bat and walk to home plate. With your knees and elbows bent, you take a couple practice swings across the plate.

The pitcher pitches the ball toward the catcher's special glove, called a mitt. You watch the ball carefully and take a level swing. WHACK!

10

The pitcher tries to throw the ball over the plate and between the batter's knees and chest. This area is called the strike zone. If the pitch is in the strike zone and the batter swings and misses, or doesn't swing at all, the umpire calls a strike. If the pitch is out of the strike zone and the batter doesn't swing, the umpire calls a ball.

The ball connects with your bat and
bounces between first and second base.
You drop the bat and run to first base
as fast as you can. You're safe!

Cori is up next. She swings at the first
pitch and misses. "Strike one!" the
umpire yells. She swings at the second
pitch and misses. "Strike two!"

When batting, keep your eye on the pitch and watch the ball as it comes toward home plate. Keep your swing level. If your bat swings upward, the ball will pop straight up into the air, making it easier for the other team to catch.

The Cardinals' pitcher throws the next pitch. Cori swings and hits the ball over the third baseman's head. You run to second base, and Cori makes it safely to first.

Jon is up next. Unfortunately, he hits a fly ball right to the center fielder. The ball's caught. You and Cori stay on your bases.

If a fly ball is hit when you are on base, wait to see if anyone catches it. If someone does, the batter is out. You can run to the next base only after the catch is made and you touch, or "tag," your base. This is called "tagging up." Run only if you can make it to the next base without being tagged out.

A hit is called a foul ball when it goes to the right of the first base line or to the left of the third base line. It is considered a strike. However, if there are already two strikes on a batter, and he or she hits a foul ball, the count stays at two strikes.

Your team has one out. James grabs a bat and gets ready to hit. He hits a ground ball to the second baseman, who tags Cori for an out. James makes it safely to first base. You advance to third.

With two outs, it's Hannah's turn to bat. She makes contact with the first pitch, but the ball rolls to the right of first base. "Foul ball!" the umpire yells. Strike one.

Hannah swings at the next pitch and misses. The count is 0 and 2. One more strike and she's out. "C'mon, Hannah!" you cheer from third base. "Bring me home!"

Hannah watches the next pitch carefully and swings as hard as she can. WHACK! The ball flies high into left field, over the other players' heads. It hits the ground before anyone can catch it.

The count is the number of balls and strikes a batter has while at bat. Balls are always said first. For example, if the count is 1 and 2, the batter has one ball and two strikes.

You turn and sprint toward home plate. The left fielder throws the ball to the third baseman, who throws it to the catcher. You touch the plate with your foot before the catcher can tag you. "Safe!" the umpire shouts.

You scored! The Muskrats are ahead, 1-0, but there's still a lot more softball to play!

Diagram of a Softball Field

Key:
Softball Positions

P	Pitcher	L	Left Fielder
C	Catcher	CF	Center Fielder
1	First Baseman	R	Right Fielder
2	Second Baseman	RB	Right-Handed Batter
S	Shortstop	LB	Left-Handed Batter
3	Third Baseman		

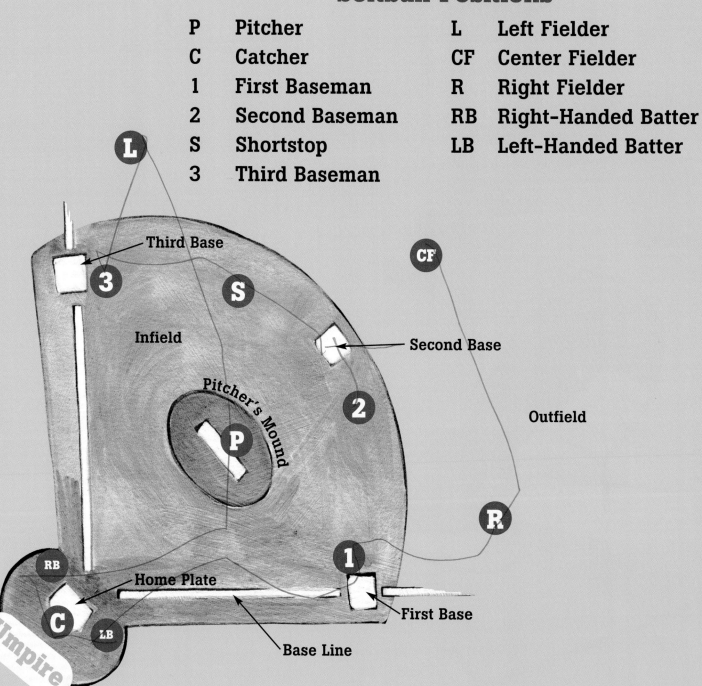

Third Base

Infield

Second Base

Pitcher's Mound

Outfield

Home Plate

First Base

Base Line

Umpire

FUN FACTS

Softball was invented in Chicago in 1887 by George Hancock. He wanted to create an indoor winter alternative to baseball. Hancock tied a boxing glove into the shape of a ball and used a broom handle as a bat.

A softball isn't really "soft." It's almost as hard as a baseball. But a softball is bigger than a baseball. It's about 12 inches (30 centimeters) around, whereas a baseball is 9 inches (23 cm) around.

Softball became an official Olympic sport at the 1996 Summer Olympics in Atlanta, Georgia. Since then, the U.S. women's softball team has won three gold medals, in 1996, 2000, and 2004.

The National Softball Hall of Fame is located in Oklahoma City, Oklahoma.

GLOSSARY

ball—a pitched ball that is out of the strike zone and not swung at; a count of four balls allows a batter to advance to first base

fly ball—a ball that is hit high into the air

ground ball—a ball that rolls on the ground after it is hit by the batter

infield—the area of a softball field that includes home plate and all three bases

inning—a period of time during a softball game in which each team gets a turn to bat until they get three outs

outfield—the area of a softball field beyond first, second, and third bases

strike—a pitched ball that is swung at and missed, a pitched ball that is in the strike zone but not swung at, or a pitched ball that is hit foul; three strikes make an out

umpire—an official person who makes sure the game is played correctly and fairly

TO LEARN MORE

At the Library

Bonney, Barbara. *Softball—Batting*. Vero Beach, Fla.: Rourke, 1998.

Nitz, Kristin Wolden. *Play by Play: Softball*. Minneapolis: Lerner, 2000.

Sublett, Anne. *The Illustrated Rules of Softball*. Nashville: Ideals Children's Books, 1996.

On the Web

FactHound offers a safe, fun way to find Web sites related to this book.
All of the sites on FactHound have been researched by our staff.
http://www.facthound.com

1. Visit the FactHound home page.
2. Enter a search word related to this book,
   or type in this special code: 1404811524.
3. Click on the FETCH IT button.

Your trusty FactHound will fetch the best sites for you!

INDEX

Look for all the books in the Game Day series:

Batter Up! You Can Play Softball

Bump! Set! Spike! You Can Play Volleyball

Face Off! You Can Play Hockey

Jump Ball! You Can Play Basketball

Nice Hit! You Can Play Baseball

Score! You Can Play Soccer

Tee Off! You Can Play Golf

Touchdown! You Can Play Football